Negotiating Your
Power Dynamic
Relationship

NEGOTIATING YOUR POWER DYNAMIC RELATIONSHIP

Raven Kaldera

Alfred Press
Hubbardston, Massachusetts

Alfred Press
12 Simond Hill Road
Hubbardston, MA 01452

Negotiating Your Power Dynamic Relationship
© 2020 Raven Kaldera
ISBN 978-0-9905441-6-6

Cover Illustrations of Hands:

http://www.macrovector.com
http://www.freepik.com
Danilo Sanino http://www.danilosanino.com
Angelo Bonavera

Printed in cooperation with
Lulu Enterprises, Inc.
860 Aviation Parkway, Suite 300
Morrisville, NC 27560

Dedicated to all the long-time members of MAsT Massachusetts, for your support, compassion, kindness, and all-around awesomeness. We are fortunate and honored to know you. Thanks especially to Drew and his Anne, Acknowledgments also to Devyn Stone, author of "A Quick Reference Guide To The Areas Of Control", who filled in a few more holes as well. Thank you all for your generosity and dedication.

Contents

Introduction

Master. Slave. Lots of people thrill to the words, probably because they've read them so many times in erotic novels, of the softcore or hardcore variety. Not everyone wants to live in an entirely egalitarian relationship; some of us thrill to the idea of being in charge or being under a trusted person's control. People who enjoy this may refer to themselves in many different ways: Dominant and submissive (D/s), Master and slave (M/s), Owner and property (O/p). Those terms have come out of the power exchange subdivision of the BDSM demographic. Terms that are sometimes used by non-BDSM folks who are practicing conscious hierarchical relationships but don't feel comfortable among BDSM folks include "leader and follower" and "leader and subordinate".

Those labels, however, mean different things to different people. The next chapter consists of an essay about the current confusion around these terms, and the array of meanings you may run into when you go looking, online or in person. We strongly suggest that you read it before you go on to the rest of this book. It may be the first step in figuring out how to put words to what it is that you want—and what words you don't want to use.

Fantasy erotic novels are wonderful, but they don't give people realistic information about how to do this sort of thing every day. In the stories, the slave is never having menstrual cramps, or pulled a calf muscle walking the dog, or worked all day at a thankless job and is ready to collapse by evening. The master never has sciatica or erectile dysfunction or small children that demand attention at the worst times. (They're also usually extremely wealthy.) In the stories, no one ever has screaming toddlers or elderly parents or grumbling roommates about, and the dramatic sex scenes are never interrupted by a late-night call from a friend asking to be rescued from a breakdown on the road, or someone's mother checking in. In real life, though, the power dynamic needs to fit in around—and in some cases, encompass—all the irritations and responsibilities of ordinary life.

Yet so often we see couples who start a power dynamic relationship with stars in their eyes, and the only things they think to bring up during the initial discussions are the sexy and/or romantic things. Months down the road, they are asking questions like, "Do I/they have the right to expect that?" We ask, "What did you two negotiate?" and they respond, "We never thought to talk about that stuff!" This happens so often that we decided to do something about it.

That's where this book comes in. It's for the absolute beginners, the people who have just begun to talk about beginning a power dynamic relationship and aren't sure what questions even to ask. Some couples will have met only recently—perhaps attracted by the other one's interest in unequal relationships—and some will have been together for years before deciding to leap in. While people in long-term established egalitarian relationships already know a lot about each other and probably already have established ways for handling everything, this book may remind them of all the myriad areas they are used to handling things in an egalitarian manner, and it may never have occurred to them that it could be done differently.

We strongly suggest that you go through this book as a couple, comparing answers with each other. While the book can also be useful for someone single who wants to scope out the territory and think about their future answers when they find someone, when there are two people involved, both parties need to put the time and energy into these answers. In fact, refusing to discuss many of these issues could be construed as a warning sign. Perhaps the other person isn't really ready for a long-term relationship, or for a power dynamic that extends beyond sexy stuff in the bedroom. If so, it may be best to limit it to play for now, and think about this later. But one person giving their answers while the other refuses to discuss things, especially when it comes to fairly crucial issues, is not going to work. Communication needs to go both ways for a power dynamic, and it needs to be clear and timely and not keep anyone in the dark. If that isn't happening now, in the negotiation stage, it bodes ill for a future time when one person has less recourse and the other more responsibility.

Another point we need to make is that there are no wrong answers. Each person should honestly say what they want, and if the lists are radically different ... well, sometimes people are just a poor fit with each other. The problem is that power dynamic relationships require a higher level of "fit" than egalitarian ones. This is because the higher the initial compatibility, the less the s-type needs to sacrifice. That said, it's perfectly OK to go through this book and decide that 90% of the questions are answered with, "No way, that's staying the way it is now, we're not involving it in the power exchange." There is no "right level" of power dynamic intensity. Everyone will create their own custom-built relationship that reflects their own mutual needs. The only "right amount" is what works for both of you.

Some couples will involve only a few items in this book in the power exchange; others will go further. A few may hand over everything, but we should emphasize that this is rare, and it is not required unless it's what you both really want. It's all right to set mutual limits. It doesn't mean that your relationship is "less than" or that you need to hand over a certain amount of authority to "earn" a particular title. Use the titles any way you like. Set the limits anywhere you both want. There is no question in here that must be answered "Yes, go for it!" in order to be involved in power exchange, and there is no label that is worth compromising yourself for.

It's also perfectly all right to look at a question and say, "Not now, but we won't say never. Let's check back on this one after a year or so." Power dynamics can wax and wane due to outside circumstances. Sometimes the s-type needs to be given more freedom if either party becomes ill or incapacitated, temporarily or permanently, or has to be absent for a time, or has to take on extra unexpected responsibilities. Sometimes the relationship progresses to levels of ownership that neither party thought they would have wanted in the beginning. It's all right to table an issue until you know how things are going to turn out.

We advise people to take it slow. Add one area of authority at a time, perhaps one every couple of weeks after you've both gotten used to the last one. (That isn't just the s-type getting used to remembering to do or not do an activity, it's the M-type getting used to remembering that they're supposed to check on it periodically.) It's more satisfying, and more functional, to be given complete authority over a small number of areas as opposed to a half-assed, spotty authority over many areas.

Also, although we've thrown in the occasional "How does the s-type feel about this?"—really, we intend for the s-type to add in an unwritten question of "…And how do I feel about this?" after every question that is answered Yes or No. And yes, that goes for the M-type too. Discuss and share feelings about each one.

At the end of this book is a list of further reading. Once you've figured out what you each want, and roughed out boundaries you're both comfortable with, you can get more information on how to manage these imbalances skillfully. We wish you luck and joy in your new venture with each other! Be thoughtful, go slow, and listen to each other, and welcome to the world of artfully unequal partnerships.

Conflicting Boundaries: Power Dynamic Role Definitions

On any forum that discusses the subject of D/s, M/s, and O/p lifestyles, it seems like a third to a half of the disagreements and misunderstandings occur because of conflicting definitions of what those labels mean ... and no awareness that there are other widely-used definitions as well. Since there have not been any statistical studies on the definitional divisions in the demographic of people who self-identify with any of these terms—not to mention in the greater BDSM demographic—I'll just say that I have seen enough personal and anecdotal evidence to believe that all of the definitions I will provide below are widespread enough in their own right to be considered a force to be reckoned with.

The problems come when those forces collide. In any given community—and there's a reason why I'm not referring to the M/s "community"; it's a multitude of (often radically differing) communities in a larger demographic that do not all share the same ideas—there will usually be one of the following definitions that wins by greatest numbers, but shifting communities generally mean shifting numbers. In some support groups or conferences, or in some online forums, the issue is dealt with by having a "house" definition that people must utilize or be reprimanded; in some there may be a rule against definitional discussions in order to preserve some amount of peace.

My point in providing these definitions is to spread awareness of the issue and encourage people to think first, before starting in on a war of "You're Doing It Wrong", that perhaps a clash of definitions is the underlying problem. It is also to provide information and options to those people just dipping a toe into the ocean of power exchange, who are concerned that the words they use aren't correct for what they want, or that they are not a "real" (fill in the blank).

First, let's look at the terms "dominant" and "submissive". I can pick out four separate definitions of these words. They are:

❖ Submissive = Bottom in a BDSM scene, or perhaps (for those who are being more specific) a bottom in a BDSM scene who enacts psychologically subordinate behaviors during the scene, as opposed to a sensation bottom who is incorporating no roleplay, or a dominant bottom who is ordering someone to give them sensation, and instructing them in how to do it. (Yes, there are such people.) For this definition, Dominant = Top in a scene who incorporates the opposite set of behaviors into the BDSM.

❖ Submissive = Person who is in the subordinate role in a limited power exchange relationship, where there is some real authority given over outside of a BDSM scene, but most of the submissive's life is their own to manage. Where is the line drawn? That is entirely subjective and up to the people in question to define, and that's why there are so many arguments. By this definition, Dominant = Person who is in the leadership role in this limited power exchange.

❖ Submissive = Person who is in the subordinate role in a quite comprehensive power dynamic relationship, where most if not all of the areas of their life are under the authority of another person … but they have a serious problem with the word "slave"; it makes them uncomfortable, so they use "submissive" instead. In this definition, Dominant equals the person on the other side of this power dynamic.

❖ Submissive = An adjective describing a personal quality; Dominant is defined the same way. The saying goes, "People are dominant or submissive; relationships are something else." This definition does not use these words to define relationship structures.

There are (at least) three different definitions of the words "master" and "slave" going on in the M/s demographic at large. Actually, there are more than three if you count the BDSM demographic, but I'm not at this time going to address the kink definition of "slave" as "person who bottoms for one scene and proclaims themselves a slave during that time". (Although if you are working largely in the greater kink demographic, you might want to keep that definition in mind as well.) They are:

❖ Slave = Person with a specific combination of (usually but not always submissive) personality traits and deep desires. They want to live their relationships in the s-type role, regardless of whether they are in a relationship or not. This definition is *personal* rather than *relational*. Similarly, Master = Person with a specific combination of (usually but not always dominant) personality traits, and a deep desire to be in that role in a relationship. I am not going to attempt to define the specific personality traits here, because they vary widely depending on who is speaking.

❖ Slave = Person who is actually in a power dynamic relationship where both parties refer to it as M/s, usually a comprehensive power dynamic where the master has real-life authority over many or most of the areas of the slave's life. (The same as the third definition of "submissive", confusingly enough.) The slave has chosen to be in an s-type role, and while they could leave (and ideally would if things did not work out, they are heavily invested. This definition is *relational* rather than *personal*, rather like the words "husband" and "wife"—you can't be a husband, for example, while unmarried, or at least not in any committed relationship. Similarly, Master = a person who is actually in a power dynamic relationship where both parties refer to it as M/s. Different people who fall into this category (or have partners who do so) draw the sub/slave and dom/master line in different places, usually with regard to full/part-time, or level of obedience, or the extent of the master's authority in the slave's life.

❖ Slave = Person who started out as the last entry, but has been conditioned over time (usually deliberately by the master, sometimes just slowly and inadvertently through constant reinforcement, to be psychologically unable to leave. While nothing is physically stopping them, their own minds have become solid chains that prevent them from (in some cases even thinking about) leaving, and in some cases disobeying. (Note: This sort of thing takes years to even get a solid foothold, so there is plenty of time to notice incompatibilities and leave.) This is also a relational definition, but it draws the line at the point where the conditioning takes hold and the slave no longer has recourse. In this definition, Master = someone who owns a slave of this sort.

Obviously, people using these different definitions are going to have different responses to the question of "what is a *real* slave or master?" People in category #3 might feel that if the slave can leave, then the enslavement isn't fully in place; people in #1 and #2 would fervently disagree with that definitional line, and tend to be resentful of those who draw the line somewhere they aren't going. They might also loudly disbelieve that the #3 category exists, which makes the individuals in the #3 category upset that their reality is not being acknowledged. People in #2 and #3 might see people in the #1 category as delusional wannabes, to which reaction individuals in the #1 category will probably react angrily.

Some people use the term "property" (thus O/p) for those in #3, leaving "slave" for #1 and #2 and avoiding arguments. The O/p term was coined in Europe by those who felt that "master" and "slave" were no longer specific enough. However, "property" is also claimed by individuals in all three categories, so it can no longer be assumed to have a universal definition either.

If we are ever to get our collective heads together as a demographic, we need to understand these conflicting definitions, be patient with them, and learn how to politely ascertain what definition someone is using. We also need to learn not to argue with them about how it is wrong, because the individual you are facing down probably has a deep emotional attachment to their definition. But so much misunderstanding and "You're Doing It Wrong" comes from not comprehending the fact that there are multiple widespread definitions, each too widespread to "stamp out" or force people to disavow.

I do agree with people who have said that we need more words, but the words "master" and "slave" are so emotionally loaded that I doubt anyone who uses them would be willing to put them down. In the meantime, our best bet would be to perhaps find auxiliary words to describe the different definitions (all of them respectful, please) and courteous, non-judgmental ways to ask someone which they follow.

Who and What Are You?

❖ Why do you want to be the subordinate partner in a relationship? What do you believe it will do for you?

❖ Why do you want to be the dominant partner in a relationship? What do you believe it will do for you?

❖ Where did you learn about your desired role? Fiction? Pornography? Have you read anything non-fiction by experienced individuals who have done this in real-time for years?

❖ Have you spoken to any real people in power dynamics, face to face? If not, why not? Could you arrange this? (We recommend the support organization MAsT—Masters And slaves Together. There are chapters in many places. If there are none where you live, consider reaching out to the MAsT website—*www.mast.net*—and asking for potential contacts in your area.)

❖ Have either of you been in power dynamic relationships before? How successful were they? What mistakes were made? Why did it end?

❖ Are either of you married (to someone else)? How does this person feel about this potential relationship? Have you all met together and talked about it, or at least all exchanged group emails about it? *(We strongly caution against getting involved with a married person whose spouse does not know about what you are doing. This almost always goes very badly. Honestly is the best policy. It's very easy for people to hide all sorts of things from each other, and then suddenly they disappear and stop returning emails, because the spouse found out, and the other person is bereft and left in the cold, perhaps never knowing what happened. Don't risk it. If you want to be polyamorous, read the polyamory chapter and check the resources in the back.)*

❖ If you are not married, are you in a committed relationship? Is it a power exchange or is it egalitarian? *(See above entry.)*

❖ Do one or both partners have children? *(See the section on Children.)*

❖ What is the M-type's ideal of the perfect submissive or slave? *(Make a list or write an essay.)*

❖ What is the s-type's ideal of the perfect submissive or slave? (Make a list or write an essay, and then compare it to the above list or essay.)

❖ What is the M-type's ideal of the perfect dominant or master? *(Make a list or write an essay.)*

❖ What is the s-type's ideal of the perfect dominant or master? (Make a list or write an essay, and then compare it to the above list or essay.)

❖ Obviously neither of you are perfect, but hoe close does each partner feel that they are to the two lists concerning their role in the relationship? Where do each of you feel that you have the most work to do to improve?

❖ What models of power dynamic relationships inspire each of you? "Old Guard" Leather? Victorian or ancient Roman servant and master? Medieval liege-fealty? Parent/child? 1950's housewife? Gorean master and slavegirl? Frodo and Sam? Military models? Superhero/sidekick? *(Make lists and compare.)*

❖ If you break up (it's possible) how do you want this to end? How would you prefer this to go in order to be as kind and fair to both people as possible?

Location and Travel

❖ Is this relationship intended to stay long-distance indefinitely, or do you eventually intend to meet in person? If not, why not? *(For long-distance relationship questions, see the next section.)*

❖ Are you both citizens in the same country?

❖ How close do you live to each other?

❖ Is it practical to visit each other on a regular basis? How regularly?

❖ Who will do the traveling? Will you switch off?

❖ Who will pay for the travel?

❖ Do you both intend eventually to move in together? What is the ideal timetable for that?

❖ What steps will you both take in order to achieve that goal? What is the timetable for those steps?

❖ Will the s-type be moving in with the M-type, or vice versa? (It isn't always the s-type who does the moving. Some s-types might have nicer homes, or lucrative careers that require them to stay where they are.)

❖ If you move in together, what personal items will the s-type be allowed to keep? Everything? Only some things? (Contrary to popular belief, most s-types end up needing a lot more things to maintain themselves than an idealistic M-type might imagine.)

❖ What contingencies will be made for the s-type should the relationship break up in less than two years? (Suggestions: If the s-type quits their job, money should be put aside for them in an account that the M-type has no access to. If they must abandon their important bureaucratic papers, these could be given to a trusted friend to hold onto in case the relationship ends. They should never be left with no resources.)

❖ If one partner decides to move to join the other one, and wants to continue working, will there be appropriate employment in that area? How long do they need to determine this?

❖ Once a power dynamic relationship is begun, will the s-type be allowed to take long trips alone? What rules will be set around where they can go and for how long, and how often they must check in?

❖ Will the M-type be taking long trips away without the s-type? How will this affect the dynamic, especially in the early stages?

Long Distance Relationships

❖ How long do the two of you intend your relationship to be long distance?

❖ Are you both comfortable about that decision?

❖ In the event that one person decides this will never be an in-person relationship, is the other person comfortable with their reasons for this decision?

❖ Do both partners feel certain that the other person is being honest with them? On what do you base this opinion?

❖ What are both parties willing to offer as proof that they are being honest about what is said online? (Obviously one can't necessarily offer objective proof of emotions, but one could find ways to give proof that one's life situation is what they say it is.)

❖ How will the s-type prove that they are following the M-type's orders?

❖ How will the M-type give the s-type a way to communicate with them quickly in the event an order needs an emergency countermanding due to outside circumstances? (*If this will not be possible, the M-type can refrain from giving an order that might require an emergency countermanding, or else let the s-type make their own decisions in the moment and simply report in with their actions and motivations.*)

❖ How will correction for errors be handled long distance?

❖ How will emotional support be handled long distance? (S-types often need a fair amount of emotional support, especially during the early phases. M-types often underestimate how great a gap is the lack of physical touch or affection in psychologically establishing a power dynamic. They will require a lot more verbal support to make up for it. Some long-distance M-types actually send a physical item for them to hold for emotional support.)

❖ How much time and effort does the M-type believe they will need to offer for a long-distance power exchange? How will they check to find out if this is reasonable? Are there other M-types you could correspond with about this? *(We ask this question because all too often we've seen M-types drastically underestimate how much time and effort it takes to maintain a power dynamic without physical presence, and when the s-type does not find it to be enough, the M-type becomes upset, labels the s-type as needy, and possibly dumps them, when the fault lay in the M-type's underestimation of what this would take. Remember that power dynamics require more relationship skills than egalitarian partnerships, not fewer.)*

❖ Will either of you be acknowledged as an "official" partner to other people while the relationship remains long distance? Under what circumstances would that not happen?

❖ If one of you finds another partner who is local, what will happen to your relationship?

Character: The M-Type

❖ What experience do you have leading people in daily-life situations?

❖ Have you ever been the full-time parent of a young child? Have you taken care of children who are not your own?

❖ Do you have M-type friends whom you can ask for support or advice? Are you a member of a power exchange support group?

❖ Do your friends consider you to be a generous person?

❖ What is your code of honor? (If you don't have one, you might look into creating one.) If you have one, do you actually follow it, or do you have trouble with that? What do you do to make it up when you slip?

❖ What are your highest values? Are they something you learned from your upbringing or something you worked out on your own?

❖ Are you good at clear, concise, honest communication, or do you tend to fall down on one or more of those points?

❖ How comfortable are you with real-world power dynamics? Are you comfortable being around people who have power over you (e.g. police, judges, bosses) or people who are serving you (e.g. waitstaff, cashiers, employees)? How you do act around them?

❖ What are your worst faults? Include the ones you are most embarrassed by or ashamed of.

❖ When confronted on faults and mistakes, how do you generally react? Do you react maturely even when the person doing it is being rude and unpleasant?

❖ How does apologizing make you feel? Do you have trouble doing it?

❖ How do you take responsibility for your actions, your decisions, and the problems Life hits you with, in your everyday life? Give examples.

❖ What areas of life are difficult for you to take responsibility when you get there?

❖ Would people consider you a reliable person? When you say you will do something, how often do you fail to come through? What is the usual culprit? Forgetfulness? Overcommitment? Shifting priorities? Fear? Inconsideration? Distraction? Lack of attention span? Overestimating abilities?

❖ Are you comfortable with the full range of your emotions? Do you feel the need to hide or repress them?

❖ Do you have serious trust issues? Would these interfere with your ability to trust someone unless they go far above and beyond?

❖ What is your support system like? (Friends, family, therapist, social or interest or religious or political groups, etc.)

❖ Do you have a habit of trying to rescue people in distress? How has that worked out for you?

❖ How much physical affection do you need? Do you expect this relationship to supply that?

❖ Is your life in good order, or are you struggling with constant crises?

Character: The S-Type

❖ What real-life experience have you had with serving people? Have you ever worked a service job?

❖ Have you ever worked a job where mistakes are absolutely not acceptable, such as health care or law enforcement?

❖ Do you have good impulse control? Are you good at motivating yourself to do what needs to be done?

❖ Do you tend to argue with your bosses at work?

❖ Do you have s-type friends whom you can ask for support or advice? Are you a member of a power exchange support group?

❖ Do your friends consider you to be a generous person? Are you a "helpful helper"?

❖ Do you have trouble setting boundaries? Do you allow people to take advantage of you?

❖ What is your code of honor? Do you believe that the s-type doesn't need one? If you have one, do you follow it firmly or do you have trouble? What do you do when you slip?

❖ Would you rather be being productive, or relaxing?

❖ Are you good at clear, precise, honest communication, or do you tend to fall down on one or more of those points?

❖ What are your worst faults? Include the ones you are most embarrassed by or ashamed of.

❖ How do you take responsibility for your actions, your decisions, and the problems Life hits you with, in your everyday life? Give examples.

❖ What areas of life are difficult for you to take responsibility when you get there?

❖ Would people consider you a reliable person? When you say you will do something, how often do you fail to come through? What is the usual culprit? Forgetfulness? Overcommitment? Shifting priorities? Fear? Inconsideration? Distraction? Lack of attention span? Overestimating abilities?

❖ Are you comfortable with the full range of your emotions? Do you feel the need to hide or repress them?

❖ Do you have serious trust issues? Would these interfere with your ability to trust someone unless they go far above and beyond?

❖ What is your support system like? (Friends, family, therapist, social or interest or religious or political groups, etc.)

❖ How much physical affection do you need? Do you expect this relationship to supply that?

❖ How much acknowledgment, approval, and appreciation do you need for doing what you are told? What is the most effective form of these positive reinforcements for you?

❖ Is your life basically in good order, or are you constantly struggling with crises?

❖ If the latter, do you hope that getting into a power dynamic will help that situation?

Daily Life

❖ What will the s-type's daily routine look like, ideally? (Separately, the two of you should construct a picture of what that would look like, and then compare pictures. If they are very different, you have a lot of work to do. Remember to add in outside-world disruptions like jobs, children and visiting family members.)

❖ How much of the day will the s-type spend under the M-type's direct supervision, and how much on their own recognizance?

❖ How much alone time will the s-type get? Daily and weekly?

❖ Will the s-type be allowed to have hobbies? Are there any hobbies the s-type currently has or would like to try that would seriously inconvenience the M-type? Would the M-type forbid those hobbies?

❖ Will the s-type be allowed to seek out interest groups? Will the M-type be allowed to veto them?

❖ Do the partners intend to have a social life together? Do they intend to be part of a kink or power exchange support network?

Service

❖ Is the s-type more interested in serving or being controlled? Is the M-type more interested in being served or controlling someone? (*Service-oriented slaves love to serve and would do it anyway; they're looking for an honorable and safe place to put that urge; they may not be all that interested in micromanagement or being locked in a cage. Control-oriented slaves love to feel held and dominated, and may not be all that interested in service, except as a form of obedience. Some masters are very interested in being served, with a competent servant who works well without supervision; others want to make someone dance like a puppet and revel in control. While many masters and slaves like both service and control, most will fall to one side or the other in preference, and it works a lot better for compatibility if both of you are on the same side.*)

❖ What work ethic was the M-type raised with? The s-type? Is there a difference that may cause a conflict?

❖ How many hours a week will the s-type spend doing work for the M-type?

❖ What services does the M-type want the s-type to offer? What services does the s-type want to give the M-type? (If you are not sure, we strongly encourage you to check out the book **Real Service**, in the reading list in the back.)

❖ Will the s-type render personal body services (e.g. bathing, dressing, grooming)?

❖ Will the s-type render domestic services (e.g. housecleaning, cooking, handy work, gardening, etc.)?

❖ Will the s-type render crafting services (e.g. sewing, art, leatherwork, flower arranging, etc.)?

❖ Will the s-type render personal assistant services (e.g. secretarial, tech support, organization, chauffeur, etc.)

❖ Will the s-type render sexual services? Courtesan ("charming companion") services?

❖ Will the s-type render child-care or pet care services?

❖ Will the s-type render health care services (e.g. massage, medication, personal trainer, etc.)?

❖ Will the s-type render specialized professional services that support the M-type's work, career, or business?

❖ Are there services that the M-type really wants the s-type to do (or just really wants done) and the s-type hates doing them? How will this be handled?

❖ Does the s-type have specialty skills that the M-type may not have considered? Are there ways that the M-type can utilize these skills?

❖ Are the services chosen by the M-type ones that make the s-type feel good about their competence, skill, and value as a servant, or are they all skills that are difficult or unsatisfying to them? What kind of a balance will there be?

Protocols, Rituals, and Rules

❖ What protocols are you interested in instituting for your relationship? (A protocol can be defined as an "if-then"—if you are in this situation, then do this.)

❖ Will the s-type have protocols of body movement? (Example: how to sit, stand, kneel, walk with the M-type.)

❖ Will the s-type have protocols of speech? (Example: "Yes, Sir/Ma'am," at specific points in conversation.)

❖ Will both partners have special rituals that they do together that reinforce their dynamic?

❖ Will the s-type have special rituals or mantras to do themselves to remind them of who they are?

❖ Will the M-type have special rituals or mantras to do themselves to remind them of who they are?

❖ Will there be a written contract with the overarching values of the relationship? Will both partners be able to put equal insight into that contract?

❖ Will the contract be reviewed periodically? What will be the protocol for making changes to it?

❖ Will the household rules be written down anywhere, or will both partners just be expected to remember them?

Training and Education

❖ Will the M-type be doing all the s-type's training, or will they outsource some of it? Which parts?

❖ Does the M-type have any teaching skills? Would they be willing to learn some, in order to be a better trainer?

❖ How will the M-type communicate how the s-type is to interact with their home and their possessions? (It helps to do a walk-around through the house and make a list of items the s-type may be interacting with, including things like the dishes and the floor, and then type it up into a "household manual" that the s-type can refer to. Such manuals don't have to be set in stone and can be added to as things change or bring themselves to the partners' attention.)

❖ Will the s-type be learning domestic skills? Art or craft skills? Mechanical or handyman skills? Bookkeeping or secretarial skills? Massage or health care skills? Will the M-type arrange this education with friends, or pay to have the s-type professionally trained? Would the M-type be responsible for choosing the teachers/program or would they allow the s-type to choose it?

❖ Would the s-type be trained in fetish-oriented skills, sexual skills, or skills around "traditional" protocols and body movements? Or, for that matter, protocols and body movements that the M-type has created? Who would train them in these skills, and who would compensate the trainer if it is not the M-type?

❖ Does the M-type have the skills to judge the s-type's ability to learn these skills? What evidence would the M-type take as proof that the s-type is unable to manage a specific skill? Are there any skills that are deal-breakers if the s-type cannot master them?

❖ Does the s-type have any learning disabilities or other physical or neurological issues that would make learning mandated skills difficult? Is the M-type willing to learn enough about those issues to help the s-type work around them, or perhaps find someone who understands these issues to help with the teaching?

❖ Would the M-type send the s-type back to school for career advancement, or perhaps training for a different career? Who would pay for this education? Would the M-type be responsible for choosing the teachers/program or would they allow the s-type to choose it?

❖ If the s-type is already in school for a specific major/degree program, would the M-type have the authority to require them to change to a different major/degree program?

❖ Would the M-type have the authority to order them to change schools, or drop out entirely?

Career

❖ Does the M-type want authority over the s-type's career?

❖ If so, does the M-type want the right to make the s-type quit their job? To quit their entire career and perhaps train for a different one? To quit working entirely and be a stay-at-home domestic servant?

❖ Does the s-type need to work? Do they go stir crazy if they do not have an outside job? Is their career a passion that they do not want to lose? Do they want to keep working out of caution in case an external emergency appears that requires extra money?

❖ Does the M-type want the s-type to work, and bring money into the household? Does this conflict with the s-type wanting to stay home and be a supported domestic servant?

❖ How will the s-type's job hours conflict with their assigned duties? Will the M-type be given the authority to decide what hours the s-type will work? How will the s-type explain schedule changes or limitations to their boss?

❖ Is the M-type allowed to call the s-type at work? Are there an boundaries around length or subject of calls?

❖ Is the s-type required to continually check for and answer the M-type's emails while at work? Are there any boundaries around this?

❖ Are there any activities the M-type would like to mandate which would affect the s-type's job?

❖ If there are conflicts, which takes precedence—job or power dynamic? (E.g.—the M-type wants the s-type's appearance changed in a way that the s-type believes will interfere with their job.)

❖ Can the M-type require that the s-type be out as kinky or as a submissive or slave at work? How will the M-type determine if this job is a safe environment for that information? Will this information affect potential future jobs if it is well-known?

❖ If the s-type is fired or let go due to obeying the M-type's various orders, how will the M-type repair the problem? Will they pay expenses, help the s-type find another job, etc.?

❖ If the s-type is an entrepreneur, does the M-type want control of their business? Under what circumstances would the M-type take the s-type's experience over their own opinions? Under what circumstances would the s-type be allowed to overrule them?

❖ If the s-type works from home and is moving in with the M-type, will they be given the space to do their work effectively? Will they be given uninterrupted time to do their work, just as if they were leaving for an external job? Would the s-type be able to say no to requests for service if they are working?

❖ What is the M-type's career like? Will the s-type be required to support it? In what way? (Examples: Hosting meals with bosses and co-workers. Driving the M-type to work and back. Emotional support. Taking care of domestic issues in order to free up the M-type for work time. Making cookies for the company party. Unpaid behind-the-scenes assistance with actual work.)

❖ Is the s-type allowed to call the M-type at work, especially if there is a question regarding the M-type's orders or preferences? Are there an boundaries around length or subject of calls?

❖ Is the M-type required to continually check for and answer the s-type's emails while at work (perhaps because the M-type needs to check to see that the s-type is obeying orders, or the s-type needs emotional support)? Are there any boundaries around this?

❖ Does the M-type ideally eventually want to quit working and be supported by the s-type's career? How will the two of you plan for this? Are there any duties that the M-type will take on or hire out in order to lighten the s-type's load?

❖ What happens if the M-type loses their job? Is there a plan for this contingency?

Family and Friends

❖ Will the s-type be allowed to continue relations with their blood kin, as they have been doing? Will there be restrictions on their contact? If so, why?

❖ Will the s-type be allowed to travel alone to visit their blood relations?

❖ Would the M-type force the s-type to interact with their blood kin even if they did not wish to? Under what circumstances?

❖ Will the s-type expect the M-type to interact with the s-type's family? To what extent?

❖ Will the s-type be allowed to continue seeing all the friends they are currently involved with? Will there be restrictions on their contact, or where they are allowed to go together?

❖ Will the s-type be allowed to make new friends?

❖ Would the M-type require the s-type to have friendly interactions with friends of the M-type whom the s-type does not like to be around?

❖ Will the s-type expect the M-type to have friendly interactions with friends of the s-type with whom they are not comfortable?

❖ To whom will the s-type be allowed to speak of the dynamic? Any friends or family? Only specific ones? No one except for other power exchange folks? No one at all?

❖ Would the M-type ever require the s-type to discuss the power dynamic with a friend or family member to whom the s-type was uncomfortable disclosing it?

Children

❖ Does the s-type have children from a former (or current) relationship? Are they minors or adults?

❖ What will the M-type's relationship be with these children, if they are minors? Stepparent? Adoptive parent? Parent's friend? Parent's partner?

❖ How much authority will the M-type have over these children? Will that authority need to be divided with, or approved by, the other parent?

❖ Does the s-type have children from a former (or current) relationship? Are they minors or adults?

❖ What will the s-type's relationship be with these children, if they are minors? Stepparent? Adoptive parent? Parent's friend? Parent's partner?

❖ How much authority will the s-type have over these children? Will that authority need to be divided with, or approved by, the other parent?

❖ Could the s-type be required to co-parent a foster child or adopt a child?

❖ Do the two of you plan to have children?

❖ Will the s-type's reproductive function be controlled by the M-type? Will the s-type lose their say over whether and when they can be made to get pregnant, or made to sire a child? Will they lose their say over whether they can stop bearing or siring children?

❖ If an unwanted pregnancy occurs, will they have a say over whether or not it will be terminated?

❖ If a child is born and the M-type does not want the couple to keep it, does the M-type have the authority to give the child up for adoption?

❖ Could the s-type be required to use contraception?

❖ Will the M-type have final say in naming a child?

❖ Will you both have equal input into childrearing techniques and decisions, or will the M-type decide for both of you, or will the M-type leave it up to the s-type to deal with?

❖ If there are minor children in the house for any reason, how will you handle visible power dynamic issues in front of them? Will it be made clear that one member of the couple is in charge, and the other one is obligated to do what they say, or will you present a more egalitarian front to them and hide important decisions? How will you phrase commands in front of the children? *(Be aware that children are not stupid, usually, and can figure out subtle power cues. I've never met adult children who couldn't figure out who had more power with their own parents, even with an unacknowledged and supposedly egalitarian relationship.)*

❖ How will you handle making sure that your children have multiple models of adult relationships in their lives? (This is especially important if there are children who are the same sex as the s-type; it's crucial to let those children see that not all members of their sex are required to be submissive in relationships. For that matter, it's important for children who are the same sex as the M-type, because they have to learn that they are not owed obedience due to their sex in adult partnerships, or they will be in for a sad disappointment as adults.)

Pets

❖ Does the M-type have pets that with which the s-type will be forced to interact? Would the s-type be required to care for them?

❖ Is the s-type allergic to them?

❖ Does the s-type have pets? Will the M-type allow those pets to live in the house, if you move in together?

❖ Is the M-type allergic to them?

❖ Would the M-type pay for the pets' expenses—food, veterinary, etc.—if the s-type moves in and gives up their income?

❖ How much time per day, week, and month does the s-type need for care of their pets?

Identity

❖ Does your partner need to be the same religion as you? Is this a deal-breaker?

❖ Would the M-type want the s-type to convert to their religion? Would the s-type want the M-type to convert to *their* religion?

❖ Does either of you practice a faith or belong to a religious group that would disapprove of your power dynamic relationship? How will you handle this dissonance, both externally and internally?

❖ How will the situation be handled if one of you converts to another religion a decade down the road?

❖ If the M-type belongs to a religious group and the s-type does not, would the M-type require the s-type to accompany them to religious functions and be polite, not bringing up that fact that they do not practice this faith?

❖ Would the M-type require that the s-type do volunteer work for the religious organization even though they do not practice that faith?

❖ If the s-type belongs to a religious group and the M-type does not, will the M-type be expected to interact with that religious group? To what extent? What is the M-type willing to do?

❖ Can the M-type require the s-type to take on a spiritual practice such as meditation or mindfulness?

❖ Is having a partner of a specific race a deal-breaker for either of you?

❖ Is having a partner of a specific cultural background a deal-breaker for either of you?

❖ Does the M-type belong to a particular racial or cultural group whose customs and assumptions the s-type does not understand?

Will the M-type train them in these customs and assumptions, or simply have them avoid the group of origin?

❖ Does the s-type belong to a particular racial or cultural group whose customs and assumptions the s-type does not understand? Will the s-type need the M-type to learn and show understanding and appreciation of these customs and assumptions in order to fully trust them? Would the M-type be willing to be trained in these customs and assumptions, by the s-type or by someone else?

❖ Will the M-type expect the s-type to take part in cultural customs that they do not identify with, as if they were part of that group?

❖ Does the s-type hope that the M-type would be willing to take part in cultural customs that they do not identify with, as if they were part of that group?

❖ What economic class did each partner grow up in? Are they different classes, or very similar?

❖ Would the M-type want the s-type to dress and act as if they are members of an economic class that the s-type did not originally belong to? Would the M-type require the s-type to hide their economic class origins, or dissociate with friends or groups who are part of that economic class?

❖ Does the s-type hope that the M-type will dress and act as if they belonged to a higher economic class than they grew up in? Does this affect how the s-type sees the M-type's dominance?

❖ What are the M-type's political views? How do they generally vote in elections? Are they part of any political interest groups, or interest groups with a political agenda?

❖ How do these political views affect their assumptions and priorities in a power dynamic?

❖ What are the s-type's political views? How do they generally vote in elections? Are they part of any political interest groups, or interest groups with a political agenda?

❖ How do these political views affect their assumptions and priorities in a power dynamic?

❖ Will the s-type be expected to change to support the M-type's political views?

❖ Will the s-type be required to quit political interest groups that the M-type does not agree with, or refrain from joining any more in the future?

❖ Will the s-type be required to work for the M-type's political concerns, even if they do not support them? Could they be made to attend rallies, to protest, even to run for office?

❖ Would the M-type want authority over whom the s-type votes for in elections?

❖ What is the M-type's sexual preference/orientation? Do they consider it a strong part of their identity?

❖ What is the s-type's sexual preference/orientation? Do they consider it a strong part of their identity?

❖ Could the s-type be prevented from having sexual or romantic relationships with individuals of their sexual preference/orientation's target group?

❖ Could the s-type be required to have sexual or romantic relationships with individuals who are not of their sexual preference/orientation's target group?

❖ Could the s-type be prevented from openly identifying with their sexual preference/orientation? Could they be required to publicly identify with the M-type's sexual preference/orientation instead?

❖ If the M-type chooses, later in life, to change their sexual preference/orientation, will the s-type be expected to adapt their own public preference/orientation to match or harmonize with it?

❖ Does the s-type have non-permanent physical attributes (e.g. hairstyle, clothing style, piercings, tattoos, etc.) or mannerisms that are associated with a particular racial, cultural, or religious group, or a particular sexual preference, and that indicate their membership in that demographic? Would the M-type be given the authority to require that they remove or downplay those attributes or mannerisms?

❖ What is the M-type's physical sex/gender? What is their public gender presentation? What is their preferred gender, if not the same?

❖ What is the s-type's physical sex/gender? What is their public gender presentation? What is their preferred gender, if not the same?

❖ Is the s-type's gender presentation important to the M-type? Would they want authority over how that is managed?

❖ Could the s-type be required to change their public gender presentation (e.g. clothing, hairstyle, mannerisms, pronouns), or be prevented from changing their public gender presentation later in the future?

❖ Could the s-type be required to engage in private play and/or sex that shifted their gender presentation in temporary ways? What about play and/or sex that shifted their M-type's gender presentation in temporary ways?

❖ Could the s-type be required to change their physical gender (e;g. with electrolysis, hormones, implants, surgery) even if it is not part of their internal gender identity?

❖ Could the s-type be prevented from changing their physical gender later in the future?

❖ If the M-type changed their gender presentation or physical gender later in the future, would their dominance (or the entire relationship) be compromised in the eyes of the s-type?

Transparency

❖ What level of honesty—going all the way up to complete transparency—will be put in place for either partner? (*The more intense and encompassing the power dynamic, the more important that it is that the s-type be transparent to the M-type. While the M-type does not need to be transparent about everything to the s-type, it is a good idea to be completely transparent to the s-type if they have major trust issues. Even if they don't, the M-type should be transparent about anything to do with the s-type, with the relationship, and with any personal issues that might affect the relationship.*)

❖ How does the M-type intend to earn the s-type's trust enough for the s-type to be comfortable being completely honest about anything the M-type asks?

❖ What is the M-type's projected timetable for earning this trust? Is there a time or a point by which the M-type will expect to have complete transparency?

❖ Will the M-type be able to refrain from becoming defensive or angry when the s-type is honest and says something that is hurtful to the M-type's feelings? (*Meeting honesty with an unpleasant emotional reaction does not positively reinforce future honesty.*)

❖ How does the s-type intend to earn the M-type's trust enough for the M-type to be comfortable being open about their intimate and vulnerable feelings and experiences?

❖ Are there areas for either of you that involve promises of confidentiality with other people outside the relationship, which need to be off-limits to transparency? (*E.g. personal details of other partners or adult children, or conversations with clients.*)

❖ If this is not currently the case, and one or both of you takes on a discipline of complete transparency with the partner, what will you do if this situation arises in future? (*E.g. refrain from taking on outside partners who need that level of privacy, refrain from going into careers with privacy issues, or determine that the partner has a right to this information, but agrees not to ask for it.)*

❖ What will be the accepted protocol when a friend says, "Don't tell (your partner), but…"?

❖ Will the M-type have access to the s-type's private journals, written or online?

❖ If these journals are used for working out issues with the M-type or the dynamic, could the M-type refrain from reading them until the s-type has finished working things through?

❖ Will the M-type have access to the s-type's passwords? Which ones?

❖ Would the M-type be allowed to use the s-type's email or online accounts as a "sock puppet" in social media, directly or by ordering the s-type to write something? Would it be acceptable so long as they did not say anything detrimental to the s-type?

Correction

❖ How does the M-type intend to correct the s-type when they fail to carry out an order?

❖ How will the M-type determine whether the failure was a deliberate act of disobedience, a mistake or misunderstanding on the part of the s-type, poor communication on the part of the M-type, an honest attempt that failed due to other circumstances, a physical or mental obstacle, or forgetfulness in the midst of chaos?

❖ How will each of these different causes be handled?

❖ How will the M-type determine what form of correction is most effective on this particular s-type? How much will the s-type's opinions and beliefs be taken into account when deciding?

❖ Do you intend to have a punishment dynamic?

❖ Do you know the difference between "punishment" and "funishment"? ("Funishment" is play-punishment, often for silly or specious reasons, and the punishment itself is usually something that both the M-type and the s-type enjoys on some level—or at least that the M-type enjoys, and the s-type is pleased that the M-type is getting enjoyment from it. Example: "You were naughty and sat on the couch, so now I'll have to spank you." Regular punishment, on the other hand, is for serious offenses and neither party gets any enjoyment from it. Example: "You drove way too fast and got a speeding ticket which we can't afford to pay. You will take a temp job flipping burgers at the fast-food joint on the corner until it is paid off, and you will not be allowed to drive until then.")

❖ If real punishment is used, what will be the method? Will there be limits on this method for times when the s-type is not feeling well?

❖ If one or both of you are not comfortable with a punishment dynamic, are you aware of alternatives? (We recommend the book

Building the Team: Cooperative Power Dynamic Relationships for a teamwork rather than an adversarial approach.)

❖ Will both partners have a discussion about what went wrong and how to fix it?

❖ What errors would be deal-breakers? Would this end the relationship, or end the power dynamic, or put the power dynamic on hold until changes were made?

Conflict

❖ When you need to have emotionally intense discussions that may involve anger, fear, or other heavy emotions, do you feel that you would do better dropping out of all parts of the power dynamic, or staying firmly ensconced in the dynamic? (*People can choose in either direction. Some couples prefer stepping out of the dynamic in order to "level the playing field". Others, especially ones with a very encompassing power dynamic, feel that dropping it is destabilizing to both people's security and have discussions within structures that reinforce the dynamic.*)

❖ How good is the M-type's self-control and anger management? Do they tend to get angry easily?

❖ What problems make them angry? How do they handle this emotion?

❖ What kinds of anger expression will be acceptable for the M-type in this relationship?

❖ How good is the M-type's impulse control? Can they force themselves to stay calm and thoughtful when hurt or irritated?

❖ Does the M-type tend to react defensively when questioned or confronted?

❖ How good is the s-type's self-control and anger management? Do they tend to get angry easily?

❖ What problems make them angry? How do they handle this emotion?

❖ What kinds of anger expression will be acceptable for the s-type in this relationship?

❖ How good is the s-type's impulse control? Can they force themselves to do difficult or tedious activities without supervision?

❖ Does the s-type tend to react defensively when questioned or confronted?

❖ How do you each express yourselves when you are in pain, or angry, or distressed? Is it recognizable to each other, or are your modes of expressions so different that you can't interpret each other's strong emotions? If so, what structures will you put in place in order to discern how the other person is feeling?

❖ How will you both handle it when the s-type believes that the M-type has given them an order that is impractical and will turn out badly?

❖ How will you both handle it if the s-type believes that the M-type has given them an order that is unethical?

❖ How will you both handle it if the M-type displays poor judgment in their life, in areas that have nothing to do with the s-type, but nonetheless damage the s-type's trust in them?

❖ How will you both handle it if the M-type displays unethical behavior in their life, in areas that have nothing to do with the s-type, but nonetheless damage the s-type's trust in them?

❖ How will you both handle it if the s-type displays poor judgment in their life, in areas that have nothing to do with the M-type, but nonetheless damage the M-type's trust in them?

❖ How will you both handle it if the s-type displays unethical behavior in their life, in areas that have nothing to do with the M-type, but nonetheless damage the M-type's trust in them?

❖ How will the s-type apologize to the M-type?

❖ How will the M-type apologize to the s-type?

❖ If the situation gets serious, would you be willing to bring in third parties to mediate? What would be the warning sign for this point?

Money

Money

- Would the M-type want authority over how the s-type spends or handles their money? What would that entail? Would the M-type have access to it?

- Would the s-type be required or allowed to save money, or invest money?

- What would the s-type consider proof that they would handle that responsibility well?

- Would the M-type want the s-type to give them money on a regular basis? How much and how often? Would the M-type have to disclose or prove what was done with it?

- Would the M-type want the s-type to buy things for them on a regular basis? What and how much would it cost? Would the M-type have to disclose or prove what was done with it?

- Would the M-type want the s-type to turn over all their money, including incoming paychecks, to the M-type to use and disperse? What would that entail? Would the M-type have to disclose or prove what was done with it?

- If this happened, how would the s-type get their regular expenses paid? Would the M-type decide what would be considered a "living expense"?

- How much of an allowance or spending money for extras would they get? Would the M-type have a say over how it was spent?

- Would the s-type need permission to spend any money?

- What would the s-type consider proof that the M-type would handle that responsibility well?

❖ If the M-type is managing both people's money and there is a financial mistake or mishandling, what will they do to make it up to the s-type and regain their trust?

❖ Would both partners have a joint account? Would the s-type be allowed to take money from the account, and under what circumstances?

❖ Would the s-type be allowed to carry a bank card?

❖ What would happen if there was an emergency? Would the s-type have access to money and permission to use it?

❖ Is the M-type thrifty or are they someone who spends emotionally? How do they handle their current money? Is the s-type allowed to inspect this before agreeing to anything?

❖ What attitude towards money was the M-type raised with?

❖ Is the s-type thrifty or are they someone who spends emotionally? How do they handle their current money? Is the M-type allowed to inspect this?

❖ What attitude towards money was the s-type raised with?

❖ If both partners have differing attitudes towards money and differing priorities as to how it is spent, how will you cooperate on this issue?

❖ If the M-type spends money more freely than the s-type, will this affect the s-type's impression of their judgment?

Sex

❖ Is this relationship going to be sexual, or is it intended to be a nonsexual power dynamic? (Yes, some people do have power dynamics that are nonsexual in nature.)

❖ Does the M-type want complete authority over the s-type's sex life? How do both people interpret that?

❖ What sexual activities would the M-type require that the s-type participate in? Will their preferences be taken into account?

❖ Will the s-type be allowed to set limits on type of activities? Will the s-type be allowed to set limits if they do not feel up to sex? Or if they are not allowed to decide, will they be allowed to give the M-type information about their condition, and will the M-type take it into consideration? What will allow the s-type to trust the M-type with this decision?

❖ Will the s-type be allowed to masturbate?

❖ Will the s-type be required to masturbate? In a particular way?

❖ What about safe sex? Will the couple be creating a fluid bond? If so, what kind of testing is necessary for both to feel safe about that?

❖ Can the s-type submit to sex but not necessarily show enjoyment, or will the M-type require them to dredge up some sincere enjoyment? Will the M-type help them figure out how to do this, if it is not obvious?

Love

❖ Do both of you want a romantic love relationship? If not, what steps will you both take in order to prevent falling in love with each other?

❖ If the M-type does not want romantic love, would they be all right with familial affection?

❖ Is love the most important foundational piece of your relationship, or is the power dynamic more important? Would you continue in this power dynamic if love faded, or would you leave and seek elsewhere?

❖ What is the M-type's love language? Is it something the s-type can provide, with or without practice?

❖ What is the s-type's love language? Is it something the M-type can provide, even with or without practice?

❖ Do you both want to get married? At what point? Do either of you feel that marriage is incompatible with power exchange?

❖ Will getting married change your power dynamic expectations for any reason?

❖ Do either of you have past relationships of any kind that have left scars that might affect this relationship? How will you handle building trust over those scars?

Polyamory

❖ Is polyamory an absolute dealbreaker for either of you? (If so, it's all right to skip this section and move on. However, as polyamory is one of the top five issues we get when it comes to people changing their minds later in the relationship, you might want to remember this chapter exists in case it ever comes to renegotiating for that down the line.)

❖ Is *not* being polyamorous a deal-breaker for one of you? Which partner wants to be polyamorous? The M-type or the s-type, or both?

❖ What experience does the M-type have with successful polyamory? Unsuccessful polyamory?

❖ If there were problems with past relationships that were directly linked to polyamory, what happened, and what will the M-type do to make sure that doesn't happen again? (*Be wary of anyone who blows this off by saying they were all crazy.*)

❖ What relationship skills were learned during these situations that have are valuable and useful?

❖ Is the M-type currently in a polyamorous relationship, besides with the s-type? If so, has the s-type been able to meet and talk with the M-type's other partners?

❖ If there is no existing polyamory, does the M-type expect to have sex with other people besides the s-type? If so, how will these people be vetted? Will both partners do the interviewing of partners together, and will the s-type have a say? How much of a say—veto power, or simply preferences taken into consideration? What activities will and will not be agreed on for these people?

❖ What kind of evidence will the M-type want to know that the s-type is not acting from jealousy when they help with vetting?

❖ Does the M-type want to add serious partners to their life, or are they just looking for casual sex? If serious partners, are they certain that they have the time and attention to spare without robbing the existing relationship? How much time and attention will be given to new partners?

❖ If it is decided that the M-type will be the primary partner, what does that mean for priorities and activities? Could secondary partners evolve into primaries, and what would that entail?

❖ What would future partners of the M-type have to do in order to be admitted into a safer sex fluid bond?

❖ If it is decided that the M-type will be the secondary partner, will they be openly acknowledged as a partner, including in public? Where are the boundaries around that?

❖ Will the M-type be using safer sex during poly encounters, or will they eventually be integrated into a fluid bond? What would have to happen for that to come about? Where are the safer sex boundaries for this?

❖ Is the M-type looking for egalitarian partners, additional s-types, or another M-type to submit to? How does the s-type feel about each these options? What would the M-type's role be in relation to each of these?

❖ How will the M-type handle jealousy, or possessiveness, or envy on the s-type's part? On a new partner's part?

❖ What experience does the s-type have with successful polyamory? Unsuccessful polyamory?

❖ If there were problems with past relationships that were directly linked to polyamory, what happened, and what will the s-type do to make sure that doesn't happen again?

❖ What relationship skills were learned during these situations that have are valuable and useful?

❖ Is the s-type currently in a polyamorous relationship, besides with the M-type? If so, has the M-type been able to meet and talk with the s-type's other partners?

❖ If there is no existing polyamory, does the s-type expect to have sex with other people besides the M-type? If so, how will these people be vetted? Will both partners do the interviewing of partners together, and will the M-type have a say? How much of a say— veto power, or simply preferences taken into consideration? What activities will and will not be agreed on for these people?

❖ What kind of evidence will the s-type want to know that the M-type is not acting from jealousy when they help with vetting?

❖ Does the s-type want to add serious partners to their life, or are they just looking for casual sex? If serious partners, are they certain that they have the time and attention to spare without robbing the existing relationship? How much time and attention will be given to new partners?

❖ If it is decided that the s-type will be the primary partner, what does that mean for priorities and activities? Could secondary partners evolve into primaries, and what would that entail?

❖ What would future partners of the s-type have to do in order to be admitted into a safer sex fluid bond?

❖ If it is decided that the s-type will be the secondary partner, will they be openly acknowledged as a partner, including in public? Where are the boundaries around that?

❖ Will the s-type be using safer sex during poly encounters, or will they eventually be integrated into a fluid bond? What would have to happen for that to come about? Where are the safer sex boundaries for this?

❖ Is the s-type looking for egalitarian partners, additional M-types to submit to, or another s-type in order to be the dominant partner? How does the M-type feel about each of these options? What would the s-type's role be in relation to each of these.

❖ Will the s-type be required that have sex with other people besides the M-type? If so, whom and what activities? How will the M-type vet these potential people? How will the M-type assure the s-type's safety?

❖ If monogamy is agreed on, and many years down the road (when the s-type may have trouble leaving) the M-type wants to switch to polyamory, what will they do to help the s-type come to a good place with this? What resources can be found for them? Books, support groups, friends, mentors? (*It needs to be said that sometimes this is a deal-breaker. It's good to try to find support for it, but there is still a fair risk of this practice just not working for one partner, and that needs to be acknowledged and discussed.*)

❖ If new partners move into the house, how will that work?

❖ If there are children, how will the poly situation be handled and explained? What will be the other partners' relationship to them?

❖ If there are fights, how will conflict resolution be handled? Do either of you have experience in conflict resolution? Would you be willing to take training for that experience?

BDSM

❖ Do either the M-type or the s-type want to engage in BDSM activities as part of this relationship?

❖ What kind of BDSM experience does the M-type have? Topping and/or bottoming? What are their BDSM skills?

❖ Do they have references from people in the BDSM scene who will speak for them?

❖ Is the M-type part of any BDSM community? If not, why not? If they were and then left, why was that?

❖ What kind of BDSM experience does the s-type have? Topping and/or bottoming? What are their BDSM skills?

❖ Do they have references from people in the BDSM scene who will speak for them?

❖ Is the M-type part of any BDSM community? If not, why not? If they were and then left, why was that?

❖ What BDSM activities does the M-type want the s-type to take part in? Will the s-type be allowed to set limits on the type of activities? Will the s-type be allowed to set limits if they do not feel up to BDSM? Or if they are not allowed to decide, will they be allowed to give the M-type information about their condition, and will the M-type take it into consideration? What will allow the s-type to trust the M-type with this decision?

❖ Will the s-type be allowed to have a safe word?

❖ Will the s-type be allowed to participate in BDSM activities with other people besides the M-type? If so, whom and what activities? How will the M-type vet these potential people?

❖ Will the s-type be required to participate in BDSM activities with other people besides the M-type? If so, whom and what activities? How will the M-type vet these potential people? How will the M-type assure the s-type's safety?

❖ If the s-type engages in BDSM activities with other people, are they allowed to mix actions of dominance and submission with the BDSM, or is that reserved only for the M-type and they must keep it to sensation activities only? Where is that line drawn?

❖ Does the M-type plan to engage in BDSM activities with people other than the s-type? What types of activities? Under what circumstances (public, private)? What about in the context of teaching a class or demo?

❖ How important is BDSM to reinforcing your power dynamic? What will you do if one partner becomes elderly or disabled and cannot do BDSM the way you have done it before? How will you adapt to this?

Body Integrity

❖ Does the M-type want complete control over the s-type's body? What does this entail, in both your opinions?

❖ Would the M-type want absolute access to the s-type's body (e.g. allowed to touch anywhere, at any time, in any way)? Would the s-type be allowed to refuse any kind of touch?

❖ Could the M-type require that the s-type get tattoos, or piercings, or branding, or decorative flesh removal, or other non-surgical body modification? In high-visibility or low-visibility areas?

❖ Could the s-type be required to get existing markings or piercings removed, if the M-type doesn't find them attractive?

❖ Could the M-type require that the s-type get elective surgery (e.g. breast implants, liposuction, mole removal, etc.)?

❖ Could the s-type's bathroom use be controlled with permission? If so, is the M-type available for permission 100% of the time, or will such control only be extended in their presence?

❖ Is the s-type allowed to drink alcohol? Under what circumstances? How much? Could they be required to do it if they do not wish to?

❖ Is the s-type allowed to use recreational drugs? What kind and how much? Under what circumstances? Could they be required to do it if they do not wish to?

❖ Is the s-type allowed to ingest nicotine? Under what circumstances? How much? Could they be required to do it if they do not wish to? If they are a smoker, could they be required to quit?

❖ Would the M-type want to dictate an exercise regimen for the s-type? What kind and how often? Will the M-type be doing the same exercise regimen with them?

❖ Would the M-type pay for a gym membership and/or trainer?

❖ Would the s-type be allowed to touch, hug, or shake hands with other people? If not in every circumstance, in which ones?

❖ Will the s-type be allowed to initiate touch with the M-type (hugs, caresses, etc.)? With or without permission?

❖ Are there parts of the body—for either the M-type or the s-type—that they are ashamed of, or seriously dislike for whatever reason? How does that need to be handled? Is there a way to use the context of the power dynamic to make you more comfortable with being touched there, or to make the other person more comfortable with having to avoid touching you there?

❖ Would the s-type be required to allow touch from other people besides the M-type? Whom and under what circumstances?

❖ Does the M-type want authority over the s-type's clothing? To what extent?

❖ Could the M-type throw out all the s-type's clothing and allow them to keep only what they prefer? If so, would the M-type fund the new wardrobe? Or would the s-type be allowed to keep clothes to wear when not in the M-type's presence, or for work? Or would the M-type allow the s-type to pick out their own clothes so long as they were in certain styles?

❖ Will the s-type's clothing preferences be taken into account?

❖ If the M-type places clothing or jewelry onto the s-type's body, can the s-type remove it without permission?

❖ Could the s-type be required to wear clothing styles inappropriate for their job to work?

❖ Could the s-type be required to wear provocative clothing in public when the combination makes them uncomfortable? If so, how will the M-type protect them from unwanted harassment by onlookers, drunks, police, etc.?

❖ Will the s-type be allowed to wear underwear? How about the s-type with a functioning uterus during menstruation?

❖ Would the s-type be required to wear special garments that remind them of their submission under their outer clothing?

❖ Would the s-type be required to wear a collar? What sort? Under what circumstances would they be allowed to take it off? Would they have to get the M-type to take it off? If the s-type feels that it is of a sort that is inappropriate in some public situations, could they take it off or switch to a more subtle version?

❖ Would the s-type be required to wear any other token of submission?

❖ Does the M-type want authority over the s-type's hair? Would they require that the s-type change the color, or style, or length? Would they require that the s-type shave their head? Will the M-type take the s-type's work and family situation into account? Will their personal preferences be taken into account?

❖ Does the M-type want authority over what parts of the s-type's body are shaved or kept unshaven (e.g. facial hair, armpits, legs, genitals, etc.)?

❖ Does the M-type want authority over the s-type's hygiene?

❖ Would the M-type require the s-type to keep their nails a certain way?

❖ Would the s-type be allowed or required to wear makeup?

❖ Would the s-type be allowed to required to wear fragrance? Does the M-type or the s-type have an allergy to any fragrance? Would this be taken into account?

❖ If the s-type wears glasses, could they be required to switch to contact lenses? To use vanity contact lenses to color their eyes?

❖ Would the s-type be required to have regular enema flushes? How often? What would the M-type take as evidence that the s-type was having physical issues over this?

❖ Would the s-type be required to wear a buttplug? What size? How often? For how long? What would the M-type take as evidence that the s-type was having physical issues over this?

Diet

❖ Does the M-type want to have authority over the s-type's diet? To what extent?

❖ Will the s-type be allowed to eat what they want when they are not with the M-type, or must dietary restrictions persist no matter what the situation?

❖ If the s-type is allowed times and places where they can eat as they like, will they have to disclose what they eat to the M-type?

❖ Will specific foods be edible, but only with permission? How is the s-type to get permission if they are not in the presence of the M-type? What if they can't get hold of the M-type?

❖ Is the s-type on a special diet due to reasons of allergies, intolerances, drug interactions, or specific diseases? If the M-type wants to control their diet, is the M-type willing to study the existing dietary restrictions and take medical advice on the subject?

❖ Would the M-type require that the s-type take on the same diet or dietary restrictions as the M-type? (For example: go vegetarian or vegan, eat keto or Paleo, etc.) How will the M-type determine if a particular diet would be healthy for this person's body?

❖ Will the s-type be expected to prepare food for the M-type that they are allergic to, or object to on a moral or religious basis? (*Example: Making a Jewish s-type prepare pork products, or a political vegan to cook meat, or someone highly allergic to nuts to work with them in the kitchen.*)

❖ If the s-type visits family and will be expected to eat foods not on their current diet, how will that be handled?

Medical

❖ What is the M-type's medical history?

❖ Do they have any physical or neurological disabilities for which the s-type will need to assist them? What kind of training would the s-type receive in order to provide these services?

❖ Are they on any medications? Will the s-type be expected to interact with that medication (fetching meds, giving injections, filling med-minders, etc.)?

❖ If they miss their medications, will their judgment be impaired?

❖ Do they have any illnesses that sometimes affect their judgment if they are not handled skillfully (e.g. low blood sugar from diabetes or hypoglycemia, etc.)?

❖ Does the M-type suffer from any mental illness (e.g. depression, bipolar, etc.)? Do they suffer from PTSD? What are their symptoms? Where can the s-type learn more about these issues?

❖ If the M-type has a neurochemical illness, are they on medication for it? Do they take the medication regularly or forget sometimes?

❖ If the s-type believed that the M-type required therapy, would the M-type be willing to go there?

❖ Does the M-type have a neurological disorder (e.g. ADHD, Aspergers, etc.) which will affect their behavior?

❖ What is the s-type's medical history?

❖ Do they have any physical or neurological disabilities that will affect their ability to provide certain services? Where can the M-type learn more about these issues?

❖ Are they on any medications? If they miss their medications, will their impulse control or mood suffer?

❖ Do they have any illnesses that sometimes affect their behavior if they are not handled skillfully (e.g. low blood sugar from diabetes or hypoglycemia, etc.)?

❖ Does the s-type suffer from any mental illness (e.g. depression, bipolar, etc.)? Do they suffer from PTSD? What are their symptoms? Where can the M-type learn more about these issues?

❖ If the s-type has a neurochemical illness, are they on medication for it? Do they take the medication regularly or forget sometimes?

❖ Does the s-type have a neurological disorder (e.g. ADHD, Aspergers, etc.) which will affect their behavior? Would they need special compensation for understanding and following through with orders (e.g. making lists, needing orders expressed in a certain way, etc.)? Can they clearly state or write down their needs in this area?

❖ Does the s-type wish the M-type to have authority over their medical care? What would the s-type need in order to trust the M-type with this responsibility? Does the M-type want that responsibility, or do they feel it would be better if the s-type handled it?

❖ Could the M-type mandate therapy? Would they want to interview and select the therapist for the s-type?

❖ If the s-type becomes too mentally ill to function, will the M-type be given the power to get them into an appropriate facility for help?

❖ What rules will be put in place in the event that the M-type has a medical emergency? What tasks will be assigned to the s-type in that event? (If they are live-in partners, the s-type may be tasked with informing family and friends, interfacing with doctors and taking notes, handling bills, interfacing with insurance companies, etc.) If the s-type is not the M-type's legal partner, will they be allowed hospital visits?

❖ What will happen if the s-type has a medical emergency? What are the M-type's responsibilities in this situation? If the s-type is not the M-type's legal partner, will they be allowed hospital visits?

❖ Does the M-type want to be able to decide whether the s-type will see a doctor or go to the hospital?

❖ Could the M-type require that the s-type get surgery for a non-life-threatening medical problem when the s-type does not wish to? *(For example, requiring that they get a deviated septum altered or a joint replaced.)*

❖ Could the M-type require medication, surgery, or other medical treatment for a serious medical problem if the s-type does not agree with it?

❖ Could they prevent the s-type from getting medication, surgery, or other medical treatment for a serious problem if the M-type does not agree with it?

❖ Would the s-type be allowed to use over-the-counter medication?

❖ Will the M-type be willing to pay for the s-type's medical insurance and other medical expenses?

❖ Would the M-type require the s-type to change their organ donor status?

❖ Would the M-type require that the s-type donate blood?

❖ Will the M-type dictate who the s-type's emergency contact will be?

❖ Will either of you be giving the other one a HIPAA medical access form (or the equivalent in your country) or medical power of attorney, or any appropriate form that allows them to know about your medical records or visit you in the hospital?

❖ If something physically happens to the M-type that permanently affects their judgment or sanity (e.g. severe TBI or Alzheimer's), what is the s-type to do? Should they leave, or stay on as an egalitarian partner? Is the power dynamic done? Are there trusted outside people who can be called in to help, in case the s-type has trouble managing the M-type? (After decades of obeying, this can be difficult. It sometimes helps to have backup.)

Life and Death

❖ Will the M-type have authority over whether the s-type is allowed to kill themselves? How will they be given the power to enable that authority? *(It's something to talk about, even if it doesn't seem like it would ever come up.)*

❖ If the s-type is terminally ill and on life support, will the M-type be given the authority to direct or prevent death? Will end-of-life documents be drawn up with the s-type reiterating the M-type's wishes, or validating their authority to make these decisions?

❖ If the M-type becomes terminally ill, will the s-type be given equal powers?

❖ Does the M-type intend to make a will that leaves something to the s-type, in case they have given up their income? How will they be taken care of in the case of the M-type's unanticipated death? *(This is no casual matter. We know of masters who have died suddenly and their relatives came down, took the house, and evicted their slaves who had no legal right to be there. Do your due diligence in this matter.)*

❖ If the M-type dies, are there any trusted friends who are also in power dynamics who could be appointed to step in and help the s-type as they recover? *(Sometimes, after decades of being told what to do, it's difficult to have to decide everything for yourself in the face of terrible grief. Having a support team who understands can be a life-saver here.)*

❖ Is there any situation that you can think of where the M-type would order the s-type to kill themselves, or would actively end their life?

Recommended Reading

❖ *Dear Raven and Joshua: Questions and Answers about Power Exchange Relationships* by Raven Kaldera and Joshua Tenpenny.

❖ *Paradigms of Power: Styles of Master/Slave Relationships* by Raven Kaldera.

❖ *Power Circuits: Polyamory in a Power Dynamic* by Raven Kaldera.

❖ *Real Service* by Raven Kaldera and Joshua Tenpenny.

❖ *Building the Team: Cooperative Power Dynamic* Relationships by Raven Kaldera and Joshua Tenpenny.

❖ *The Way of the Pleasure Slave* by Andrew James.

❖ *Don't Shoot the Dog! The New Art of Teaching and Training* by Karen Pryor

❖ *Sacred Power Holy Surrender* by Raven Kaldera.

❖ *Unequal By Design: Counseling Power Dynamic Relationships* by Sabrina Popp, M.D. and Raven Kaldera.

❖ *Hell on Wheels: Disabled Dominants* by Raven Kaldera.

❖ *Kneeling in Spirit: Disabled Submissives* by Raven Kaldera.

❖ *Broken Toys: Submissives with Mental Illness and & Neurological Dysfunction* by Raven Kaldera.

❖ *Mastering Mind: Dominants with Mental Illness and & Neurological Dysfunction* by Raven Kaldera.

❖ *Where I Am Led: A Service Exploration Workbook* by slavette.

❖ *Master/slave Mastery: Updated Handbook of concepts, Approaches, and Practices* by Bob Rubel.

About the Author

Raven Kaldera is a Northern Tradition Neo-Pagan shaman, homesteader, astrologer, herbalist, vampire, and intersexual transgendered FTM activist. He is the King of a very small Pagan kingdom, and one of the founders of its current incarnation, the First Kingdom Church of Asphodel. He is the author of far too many books to list here, but can be found at his hub website, www.ravenkaldera.org. He is also the owner of an extremely competent and amazing slaveboy named Joshua. 'Tis an ill wind that blows no minds.

www.ingramcontent.com/pod-product-compliance
Lightning Source LLC
Chambersburg PA
CBHW031220290326
41931CB00035B/627